WHY WE LIVE AFTER DEATH

Books by Dr. Richard Steinpach

BIRTH AND JUSTICE
FALSE WAYS
HOW CAN GOD ALLOW SUCH THINGS
IT HAS BEEN DEMONSTRATED
THE LECTURES
"SEE THE TRUTH IS SO NEAR AT HAND..."
SELF-KNOWLEDGE
THE WAY AND THE GOAL
WHAT GOETHE WISHED TO TELL US
WHY WE LIVE AFTER DEATH

"If we go to the root of the matter, it is our concept of death that decides our answers to all the questions which life poses."

–*Dag Hammerskjöld*
Late Secretary-General of the United Nations

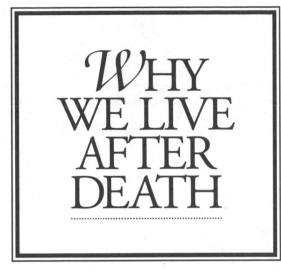

WHY WE LIVE AFTER DEATH

by Dr. Richard Steinpach

GRAIL·FOUNDATION·PRESS

GAMBIER, OHIO

Library Systems and Services Cataloging-in-Publication Data
Steinpach, Richard.
Why We Live After Death / by Richard Steinpach
p. c.m.
Includes bibliographical references.
ISBN 1-57461-005-8
1. Future life. I. Title.
BL535.575 1995 129—dc20

Cover and Book Design: Nanette Black, N. Black Designs
Typesetting: Linda Mahoney, LM Design
Printer: Malloy Lithographing, Inc.

Printed on recycled paper.

*This book contains the translation according to
the sense of the original German text.
In some cases the words of the translation can
only render the original meaning approximately.
Nevertheless, the reader will come to a
good understanding if he or she absorbs inwardly
the meaning of the contents.*

*hat matters is to enlighten people unreservedly about everything associated with death and what takes place at that time, because all this belongs inseparably to the great oneness of our existence. We shall all have to cross this threshold one day. Is it not better to do this knowingly, instead of being pushed into the unknown?*

C O N T E N T S

· ·

*B*etween 1979 and 1990, Richard Steinpach gave hundreds of lectures on various topics all over the German-speaking world. The powerful response to his lectures not only confirmed the relevance of the topics he discussed, but also compelled him to publish them in book form. Grail Foundation Press is pleased to publish Dr. Steinpach's works in America for the first time.

· ·

"Life"—a word with a thousand connotations. What does it mean? Speak of life and the impressions aroused are as myriad as the number of human beings on earth. To one person, it signifies a long and meaningless course of existence. To another, it symbolizes the enjoyment of as many earthly pleasures as possible. And for a third person, it means experiencing the wonder of the moment. Speak of "death" however, and the response is almost the same regardless of the age or condition of the listener: instant discomfort. Many will quietly leave the vicinity where this word has been spoken in an effort to distance themselves from it, as if by withdrawal they might somehow delay the inevitable.

What is the source of the discomfort aroused by a simple monosyllabic word? Why the shudder when we speak of death? For most, it is fear of the unknown. One day we will all cross that threshold—this we know, but what lies beyond for most human beings is an uneasy question, and with it fear.

Life as we know it is a continuum of experiencing. And what is experiencing? Experiencing is the inner perception of an outward impression that registers within the individual, either in a pleasant manner or in a painful manner, or sometimes in a combination of both in variable proportions. One can experience physical pain, i.e., disease or

injury, or psychic (spiritual) pain, i.e., personal loss or discomfort. In the same way, one can experience either physical pleasure or psychic pleasure, which we call "happiness"
and "joy."

In the final analysis, all earthly experiencing can be
divided into these two categories (pleasure and pain) or
some combination of the two. But what is the purpose of
all this earthly experiencing? Why do we go through the
process of being born and experiencing alternately pleasure
and pain in a repetitive cycle only to arrive at death? There
must be a purpose to it and if there is such a purpose, then
there must be a reason for the moment when it all comes to
an end.

If death signifies the end of a meaningless cycle of pain
and pleasure, then all men should naturally welcome death.
So why the fear and dread? Is it because deep inside we sense
there is a higher purpose to life on earth other than hitherto
acknowledged? Do we intuitively sense that each experience,
whether painful or pleasant, is meant to serve a deeper purpose than we were willing to recognize? Do we recognize,
after all, that we cannot blame God for the particular cir-
cumstances and experiences of our lives and that ultimately
we are responsible for our own life conditions? Do we
inwardly know that one day we will have to account for
each and every experience? Just as a school boy who has
neglected his studies and frittered away his time dreads the
final examination, so it seems many dread that final
moment of accounting when they must demonstrate what
they have gained through their experiences in the school of
life on earth.

Since the beginnings of recorded history we have celebrated birth and mourned death. This indicates the importance we place on earthly life. We have created for ourselves an impression of existence that begins with entry onto this planet and ends with our exit from it. Just as early man believed that the earth was the center of the universe around which everything revolved, so it seems that many today perceive life on earth as the focus and center of our existence. The few who challenge the existing concepts arouse only fear in the hearts of those who are thus jolted from their comfortable delusional state. Unfortunately, many religions shroud death and the beyond in mysticism. Is it possible that what we have been led to believe is not necessarily true, and therefore needs to be reexamined?

In this book, Richard Steinpach has successfully brought together two worlds that have remained separated until now: the material world of science and the ethereal world of the spirit. If man consists of more than a physical body, then he must seek to understand the connections between the real "him," which is invisible and intangible, and the outer "him," which is materially visible and tangible. Seen in this light, the question of where he goes when his physically tangible body no longer exists becomes crucial.

Dr. Steinpach demystifies the world beyond. He shows how the basic Laws of Nature, which manifest in the visible world, also take effect in the invisible—but very existent—ethereal world. He takes the extra step that has remained a stumbling block for many investigators, which is simply to apply the very same principles that activate all material processes to his investigation and explanation of ethereal processes. By basing his interpretations on what we already know about the world around us and the life we experience daily, he opens up a new vista of knowledge concerning life and death. He makes it possible to let go of the fear surrounding this inevitable event, and also brings home very clearly to the reader a sense of his own responsibility as "master of his fate" within the framework of the Laws of Creation.

Ostensibly about death, this book guides the reader to a source of immense knowledge encompassing every aspect of life and provides a starting point for living consciously from birth to death and beyond.

Dr. Ifeoma Ikenze, MD
San Rafael, California

WHY WE LIVE AFTER DEATH

*Manuscript of
a lecture by
Dr. Richard Steinpach*

hy We Live After Death is perhaps a strange sounding title, for it makes an assumption that for most people is not a certainty, namely that there is a continuation of life after death. Some people believe in it, but their ideas about it differ widely. On closer examination it appears for many to be only a matter of hope rather than a knowing conviction. Others want to demonstrate how fearlessly they face the limitation of their existence; they declare that with death everything is ended. Finally, between these two camps there are, in addition, a great number of those who, for fear of believing in something that has not yet been sufficiently proven, look upon death as a great unknown, whose incomprehensible inevitability simply has to be accepted.

But we need not continue in this uncertainty! The truth lies within our immediate reach, but only if we do not close ourselves to it!

In recent years death has been, so to speak, "rediscovered." A separate science is now concerned with dying: thanatology. Its name is derived from the Greek word "thanatos," meaning death. Outstanding among the numerous research workers using exact scientific methods in this connection has been the American doctor, Raymond Moody, whose book *Life After Life* (Bantam Books, Inc.) became a bestseller. This surely indicates that people are longing for an answer to this question. But to what extent could the numerous books published on the subject in recent years supply the answer?

Like other researchers, Dr. Moody compiled reports of the dying, including those of persons who had been declared clinically dead, and who nevertheless could be brought back to earthly existence. The interesting point here was not this medical happening, but the startling similarity of the experiences that these people had in the interval between life and death.

They were persons of various levels of education and social status. Some lived in the country, some in cities. They were of different nationalities and even from different cultures. They had diverse religious views, suffered from different diseases or injuries, and received different medical treatment. Nevertheless, as they hovered between life and death, they had passed through almost identical phases. All of them experienced initially a new state that Dr. Moody called "being out of the body." They saw themselves, or more accurately their bodies, with which they no longer identified themselves, lying on the bed or at the place of the accident. They saw the efforts of those around them and heard their words. Those persons who, according to Dr. Moody, "had penetrated more deeply into the realm of death" had the feeling of being drawn through a dark narrow passage. Then they saw a bright but not blinding light, sensed the nearness of a loving being, and experienced a "playback" of their life. Their concept of time and their knowledge had altered, expanded, and they thought they understood the true connections.

I need not concern myself here with the doubts that were raised over Dr. Moody's report on "life after life." Dr. Moody himself has adequately refuted the skeptics. I propose to deal with something else. Valuable and important as are the research findings of the thanatologists, they have only compiled descriptions of experiences. Yet they have not explained the process of dying. To understand the significance of this so important turning-point, it is essential to know how it is possible at all for us to go on living after death.

To close this gap is the purpose of this lecture. Explanations will be given here that you have not found in any of the books about dying published in recent years. Only then will you be in a position to understand and incorporate the reports compiled by the scientists. There is nothing sinister or sensational about these reports. They are fragments, on-the-spot recordings related to a happening, which you will be able to survey to a much greater extent. For death too is a completely natural process, which proceeds according to firmly established, clear and—what seems to us most important—intelligible Laws.

I should like to say in advance: the explanations you are to hear are based on *In the Light of Truth: The Grail Message* (Stiftung Gralsbotschaft, Stuttgart, Germany), a work yet to be spoken of. Already you can see that its title is justified by the fact that what is stated in it explains to us all the processes associated in the widest sense with death.

I therefore invite you first of all to receive without prejudice what I wish to present to you on the subject. When I say "without prejudice" I mean this: whenever you read or hear something that seems to you new or startling, I ask you not to protest, saying, "that cannot be," or to measure it by your own previous conceptions. Instead, I suggest that you reflect on it and examine what you have heard. You can and should conduct this examination subsequently by applying it to the facts that are known to us and to the descriptions previously mentioned.

And finally I mean by this something more: we should at last rid ourselves of the habit of regarding what is invisible as incomprehensible or even unnatural. This attitude is quite unjustified. We know only too well how inadequate are our senses. We cannot even perceive infra-red light, ultra-violet light or ultra-sonic sound. We are constantly surrounded, indeed permeated, by waves of the most diverse kinds without noticing them. It would therefore be absurd for us to deny that there are also realities beyond our senses. The very fact that we have such a concept as "the beyond" at all surely means that we are quite aware of the existence of such worlds.

For a better understanding of what is to follow, let me begin at once by defining these regions. From now on I shall refer to the earthly as the World of Gross Matter, and to the beyond as the World of Ethereal Matter. It should be understood that this is only a broad distinction, which, for the time being, disregards the stages of transition.

The first requirement for further contemplation is that we obtain clarity about ourselves, about the question, "What really is man?" The recognitions of the Darwinists, neo-Darwinists, the behaviorists, and evolutionists are indeed only half-truths, right and wrong at the same time. They are concerned only with the development of our body and its organs. But the real man is not his body. To assume so would be like failing to differentiate between the driver of a vehicle and the vehicle itself. There is within us something that is capable of being conscious of itself, which can think about itself and already distinguishes us from animals. This something can intuitively perceive not only joy and sorrow, love and hate, but also abstractions such as art, beauty, and sublimity. And with this expression "intuitively perceive," which seems to offer itself naturally here, we touch precisely upon what is actually human within us. This actual humanity is the spirit! Its voice, its language, through which it makes itself known, is the intuitive perception. It is that welling-up that does not depend on external sensory stimuli, but flows forth spontaneously from the innermost depth of our being.

With this we have found the way to the sensing, to the experiencing of our spirit. However, I find it necessary to define this concept still more sharply. Therefore listen to what is said about it in *In the Light of Truth: The Grail Message*:

"*Spirit is not wit, and not intellect! Nor is spirit acquired knowledge. It is erroneous, therefore to call a person "rich in spirit" because he has studied, read and observed much and knows how to converse well about it. Or because his brilliance expresses itself through original ideas and intellectual wit.*

Spirit is something entirely different. It is an independent consistency, coming from the world of its homogeneous species, which is different from the part to which the earth and thus the physical body belong. The spiritual world lies higher, it forms the upper and lightest part of Creation...

Spirit has nothing to do with the earthly intellect, only with the quality that is described as "deep inner feeling" ("Gemuet"). To be rich in spirit, therefore, is the same as "having deep inner feelings" ("gemuetvoll"), but not the same as being highly intellectual." . . . .

It is a sad indication of the extent to which we have already buried the spirit within us that we often confuse the spirit with the intellect. The only thing that the intellect can do, namely to connect and draw conclusions from experiences and information supplied to it, can, in limited cases, already be done today much better by computers than by us. Indeed the intellect is only an instrument bound to the body, an instrument meant to enable the spirit to manifest itself according to its nature in this earthly world.

Thus, our true ego is spirit. It is the only living thing within this earthly body that keeps it alive as such. But this spirit is not directly inside the body, for its species is too different from that of the earthly body.

Thus the spirit also has next to it finer, lighter, more permeable coverings, coming closer to it in the gradation-order of Creation, and thus also one of ethereal substance. It is this manifestation, the spirit in its ethereal body covering, which has already been seen by many clairvoyant persons, and to which the concept "soul," by which unfortunately people usually envisage so little, is applicable. The "soul" therefore is not something independent that exists side by side with the spirit; it is the spirit clothed in ethereal substance.

A positively dramatic account of the existence of such an ethereal body is to be found in the New Testament, according to which Jesus appeared to Mary Magdalene after His burial, and also several times to His disciples. He walked beside them, they spoke with Him, but did not recognize Him. He entered rooms whose doors were locked, and only when He broke bread with them at the table did they perceive that it was Jesus. This testifies quite clearly that He came to them in a different, changed bodily form, in precisely that ethereal body, which they, shaken by the deep experiences arising from the events of the previous days, were enabled to see at that time. Had it been otherwise, they would surely have recognized Him immediately. But Jesus wished by this not only to tell them that He was risen. He wished to demonstrate to them that life goes on, not only after a far-off Judgement Day, but immediately after earthly death.

Yet even the ethereal body just discussed is still too different in nature from the earthly body. Therefore, there is between this ethereal soul and the gross material earthly body another necessary transition, the so-called astral body. It comes very near to the earthly body in its consistency; the astral body is the direct prototype of the physical body, its model so to speak. It may perhaps seem strange to express it in this way.

But we know today that the minutest building-stones of our material substance, neutrons, protons and electrons, become ever less material the deeper one delves into their properties. And now consider that like all material substance, our bodies also consist only of such elementary particles. When we remember that everything which to us has the semblance of firmly-knit matter, which scientifically proven consists of radiation, of that incomprehensible something out of which the Universe at one time developed, that here an unceasing process of alternation is at work, transforming radiation into particles and particles into radiation, then it quite clearly indicates that our entire earthly world is formed, so to speak, from above downwards. It is purely and simply the result of an uninterrupted process of condensation. The existence of finer coverings, therefore, follows almost as the logical consequence of our physical world-picture. How far this world-picture can be expanded can be seen from the mere fact that, for example, only a few decades ago the recognitions of the relativity theory, quantum physics, molecular biology or radio astronomy would have been ridiculed as fantasy, occultism or superstition. Let me repeat: everything, which to us has the semblance of firmly-knit matter, scientifically proven, consists of radiation, of that incomprehensible something out of which the Universe at one time developed. Again let us consider that here an unceasing process of alternation is at work, transforming radiation into particles and particles into radiation, then it quite clearly indicates that our entire earthly world is the logical consequence of an uninterrupted process of condensation.

Therefore, let us again hold fast to these three concepts with which we will have to occupy ourselves in the following: there is, on the one hand, the gross material earthly body, also called the "mortal cloak"—after that the astral body, which in its consistency comes close to it—and finally, the spirit in its ethereal body covering, the so-called soul. Now the soul is connected with the astral body, and thereby also with the physical body, through the "silver cord," which likewise has often been seen by clairvoyant persons. It is a kind of ethereal umbilical cord. It runs into the same place as the gross material navel cord that once connected us with the womb, that is, in the solar plexus. This "silver cord" is, on sober consideration, the ethereal manifestation of the "construction-design" that we find again in the familiar umbilical cord. It is the channel for the influence of the spirit on the physical body.

You may now want to ask, "Where are these various coverings then?" Indeed they are all inside us. Yet because of their different consistencies they cannot blend with each other but only unite. They are fused into one another like the parts of a collapsible telescope, and they are held in this position, bolted as it were, by that tremendous power that holds together everything in Creation, from the greatest to the smallest. This power is radiation.

Today, we know of course from physics that everything radiates, that the apparent solidity of our material substance is due to nothing other than just this radiation, which connects the elementary particles.

Ladies and gentlemen, may I remind you in this connection of an old, well-known proverb: "Food and drink keep body and soul together." This is mainly taken as a justification of the pleasures of the table. Yet what wisdom, what knowledge of the true connections lies in it! For it is clearly stated here that body and soul are two separate things, that they are only held together, and that for this to occur a certain consistency of the physical body is necessary, the achievement of which simply requires a supply of material nourishment. If it does not receive this nourishment or if it becomes ill, then it is weakened. This of necessity means that its radiating-power, its radiation, also becomes weaker.

With this we have arrived at the decisive point. I will now give you the key to the understanding of that happening with which we are dealing. I will again do this with words from *In the Light of Truth: The Grail Message*, in which we read:

"*Thus it happens...that the soul must sever itself from a body which has been forcibly destroyed, or from one ruined by disease or weakened by old age, at the very moment when this body, owing to its changed condition, can no longer produce that strength of radiation which brings about such a magnetic attraction-power as is necessary to contribute its share in the firm union between soul and body! This results in*

10

*earthly death, or the falling back, the falling away
of the gross material body from the ethereal covering of the spirit, thus in separation. A process
which takes place, in accordance with firmly-
established Laws, between two species which
only unite at an exactly corresponding degree
of heat through the radiation simultaneously
produced, but which can never blend, and
which fall apart again when one of the two
different species can no longer fulfill the
condition laid upon it.*"

Hence soul and body must contribute their share to this
radiation connection. Of course it is generally the earthly body
wearing itself out whose radiation diminishes for one of the
aforementioned reasons; but it can also be that the connection
is severed because the radiation of the soul is no longer directed
to the earthly body with the necessary strength. These then are
cases where a human being, not suffering from any specific disease, departs this life simply because he no longer has any will
to live. There are of course also intermediate stages. If someone
does not feel well, physically or psychically, are we not inclined
to say, "He is not quite himself" or "He is not in his right
mind?" Surely these phrases quite clearly refer to a loosening of
the cohesion necessary for our full strength. Thus we read further from *In the Light of Truth: The Grail Message*:

"*Even when the gross material body is asleep
its firm union with the soul is loosened,
because during sleep the body produces a different
radiation, which does not bind so fast as that
required for the firm union. But since the union*

11

*still exists only a loosening takes place, no
separation. This loosening is immediately
ended at each awakening."* ....

This reference to sleep establishes a bridge for our understanding. Here is an experience that each of us can have every
night. Sleep has often been described as the little brother of
death. Is this only because in sleep man is removed from
active life? Or have people not, after all, been aware of the
common cause, based on the Laws of Nature?

Although man is known to spend one third of his life in
sleep, science began to apply itself to sleep research only
about two decades ago. The findings of this research are
unfortunately and generally too little known. Therefore, I
would like to tell you something about it; in this information
we already have the first possibility of recognizing the rightness of what has just been said.

We know that micro-electric processes are constantly
going on in our brain, the effects of which can be measured
as brain-current with the electroencephalograph. This brain-
current cycles up to thirty times per second in the waking
state. In sleeping persons it drops to half a cycle per second in
the course of falling asleep. At the same time the heartbeat,
respiration, blood pressure and body temperature also dimin-
ish. The body economy is maintained only on a "pilot light."
Research has established the outward signs of a reduction of
all vital functions, naturally also accompanied by a reduction
of the body's radiation, which is dependent upon the vital
functions. This, however, confirms exactly what you have just
heard. For this diminished body radiation makes possible the
loosening of the soul. Before achieving deep sleep, some persons even have the sensation that they are falling and they
physically twitch. It is the moment when the soul rises out of
the previously firm radiation-connection.

Only after reaching deep sleep does the phase of eventful dreaming begin. As sleep research has discovered, deep sleep can hardly be attained while standing or sitting. For this to happen the body needs a horizontal support, which allows one a fuller relaxed repose. Muscle and tendon reflexes have now ceased, so that occasionally even the chin drops and the person snores. Thus the body lies free of tension, like the covering of a ball from which the air has escaped. What more do we need by way of proof that here the carrying or animating support is lacking, and therefore this support is obviously of a different species from this earthly body?

While the body is thus relaxed, we dream. Sleep research has established that all human beings dream every night. Why we only sometimes remember dreams can be easily explained, but it would lead us too far from our subject. It can also be confirmed that a person is dreaming by observing that while dreaming the eyes move back and forth with remarkable speed behind the lids. This rapid eye movement, which can be measured on the oculometer, is so characteristic that it has given its name to this phase of sleep. It is called REM or "rapid eye-movement" sleep.

If the subject sleepers were awakened during this phase, they confirmed that they had just been having vivid dreams. Often, the eye-movements behind the closed lids even corresponded to the content of the dream. If someone had dreamed that he was climbing a ladder, his eyes would be looking upwards; if he dreamed that he was lifting something from the ground, he would be looking down. But nothing is to be seen from the closed lids of the earthly body. In this way research gives us evidence that our ego is something other than this body, and that this ego, the spirit, sees and experiences. During sleep the eyes of the earthly body follow these impressions only because in sleep the connection of the soul with the body is not yet severed, but only loosened. That these eye-movements take place more rapidly than in a waking state and are jerky, suggests that the spirit is experiencing a world of higher animation that the sluggish earthly eye is hardly able to follow.

Thus we find here confirmation of the fact that the change of radiation releases to us a new sphere of experiencing. It makes possible the loosening of the soul and the spirit present within this soul. What we describe as dreams are the experiences of the spirit in the world beyond.

If further evidence is needed that the radiation is decisive for union between soul and body, it can be seen in the following: sleep research has established that the phase of REM-sleep, that is the stage at which the soul has already loosened itself from the body, can be reached more quickly in a cool room. The reason is obvious: the reduced room temperature leads to a quicker decline in body temperature associated with diminished vital functions, and therefore to an earlier decrease in its radiation. Finally we are all familiar with that stage between dreaming and waking when conscious thinking is already beginning to set in, but when we are still unable to move the body. We are just bringing the "soul" near, and as long as the radiation of the body is still not strong enough, the soul simply does not have it fully "in its grip." It is like engaging the clutch in a motor vehicle.

And now, after this first example, let us turn to death. When, in the opinion of science, does it take place? The view held today is that brain-death is the decisive sign. This means the cessation of measurable brain-current on the electroencephalogram. This is in complete agreement with what sleep-research has established, and at the same time with what we have heard about the magnetic union of body and soul caused by radiation. The diminishing of the brain-current up to the attainment of deep sleep has led to the loosening of the soul. The cessation of this wave-pattern appears to medical science to be death. But what is the brain-current, other than a measurable oscillation peculiar to the body? Like all living oscillation it is a characteristic of radiation, because all radiation manifests as vibration: it is vibration. If such an oscillation is no longer measurable, this, to the doctor, signifies death. Thus you see that science strictly establishes what matters, but it sees only the fact and does not yet recognize its actual significance.

As can be ascertained during the gradual attainment of deep sleep, the decline in the body-radiation does not take place suddenly. If we disregard those cases in which the body is destroyed by violence or mutilation, then it is a question of a smooth, gliding process, as if one were slowly and steadily reducing the current of an electromagnet and finally switching it off. This explains the difficulty in accurately determining the time of death. It was formerly thought that it had set in when the respiration ceased, and thereafter, when the heart stopped. But where actually is the end? How is it possible for the "clinically dead" to be able to come back to life?

Let us take a quick glance in the opposite direction. What happens at the entry into earthly life? Here also, the medical world cannot state clearly when human life begins. For example, the most diverse opinions have been put forward on the question of abortion. Here too, the reason lies in the fact that the attracting of the soul through the increasing radiation of the developing earthly body takes place gradually until the magnetic union holds. The infallible signs of this are the first movements of the child in the womb. Only now has the soul taken full possession of the body, and is able to move it.

Thus "clinical death" also is only that moment in which the too greatly diminished body-radiation no longer allows the soul still to maintain the bodily functions at a measurable strength. Just as with entry into life, the connection with the approaching soul gradually became stronger, so also is its severance not yet finally completed at the point in time that we regard as death.

We have so far discussed the means by which death comes about, namely through the weakening of the radiation-connection. Now let us occupy ourselves with what really happens at death. Again I would like to tell you this in the words from the *In the Light of Truth: The Grail Message*:

"*At severance of the soul, this as the mobile part draws the astral body away from the physical body. Figuratively speaking: upon its exit and departure the soul draws the astral body with it out of the physical body. That is how it appears. In reality the soul only pulls it off the physical body, because there was never a fusion but only a sliding into one another, as with a collapsible telescope.*

In so doing the soul does not draw this astral body very far, because it is anchored not only with the soul but also with the physical body; and moreover the soul, from which the actual movement issues, wants to sever itself also from the astral body, and accordingly strives away from it as well.

Thus after the earthly departure of the soul the astral body always remains near the physical body. The further the soul moves away, the weaker the astral body also becomes; and the ever-advancing severance of the soul finally brings about the decay and disintegration of the astral body, which in turn immediately brings in its train the decay of the physical body, in the same way as it also influenced its formation. This is the normal process in accordance with the Laws of Creation."

Let me summarize this explanation because of its great importance: through the body-radiation having become too weak, the connection of the telescoped covering is severed; it is, so to speak, unbolted. Like a balloon that is no longer tethered, the soul, as the lightest part then floats away. As the only living thing in man, it alone was able to hold together the structure of the body in the astral sphere, as well as in the earthly gross material sphere. If the connection with the spirit is severed, these forms must disintegrate.

The passage I just read to you states that this is the normal process according to the Laws of Creation. However, the severance of the soul does not always take place so simply. I may remind you that not only is the soul kept within its denser coverings through the mutual radiation, but it has in the already-mentioned "silver cord" a direct line, a connection to the astral body, and thereby to the physical body. What is decisive for the soul, not only to slip out of its body but also to detach itself completely from it, is the condition of the ethereal soul-body and its homogeneous connection-cord. This depends entirely on the spiritual nature of the individual human being.

If through his volition a person is strongly focused on the earthly, if he did not wish to know anything about continuing life after death, of an ethereal world in the beyond, then through his own attitude, the connection-cord is very firmly knit, and will be difficult to sever. The severance may then take many days, during which time such a person, because of the density of the connection-cord, must still feel what happens to his physical body, so that, for example, he does not necessarily remain insensitive to cremation.

On the other hand, the connection-cord, in the case of a noble spirit striving for the Light, who bears within him the conviction of a continuing life, can very soon become so loose that it no longer acts as a channel for pain, and the dying person is even spared the last physical pains.

You may see from this how immensely important it is to know of these things. Your attitude to the question of death helps to decide how easy or how hard it will one day be for your soul to detach itself from your body. Also, it reveals how much harm is caused by the lack of knowledge about the process of dying. Postmortem examinations are carried out thoughtlessly in hospitals and the supposed corpses are dissected. Even worse, since the medical world has succeeded in transplanting organs it views the dying as a kind of storehouse for spare parts. Many institutions and persons in public life advocate this; indeed, they absolutely consider it a human duty to permit the removal of organs from the discarded body. There is nothing against the well-meaning motive that leads a donor to make such a disposition, although, viewed in a higher sense, it is hardly to the benefit of the one provided for. Every such donor must know what he is taking upon himself. At the time the organ is removed, which, as is well-known, must take place immediately after the presumed death if the organ is still to be usable, he is by no means "really dead," otherwise the organ could no longer be fit for use. In any case, the connection-cord is not yet completely severed. When the density of the connection-cord, depending on the nature of the person concerned, can still act as a channel for pain, such a person will still feel the infringement very perceptibly. Therefore, it is with good reason that some rites, especially among primitive races, provide for minimum intervals between death and burial, or even cremation.

The limited continuation of the connection-cord also explains how it was that the persons interviewed by the thanatologists, several of whom had indeed already been considered "clinically dead," could return to life. In all these cases the connection-cord simply was not yet severed.

This natural fact also explains the alleged miracle of the waking of the dead, thus also that of Lazarus. In this Creation nothing can take place that would not be according to its Laws. To return to earthly life is always only possible for him whose "line" between spirit and earthly body still exists, thus making re-entry possible. The miraculous in such happenings lies in the to-us incomprehensible power that causes such a return. In the cases reported by Dr. Moody, it was of an other-worldly nature; in the case of Lazarus through Jesus, even of a Divine kind.

The increasing distance of the soul from the body, and the ever greater force required to strengthen the radiation-connection again, is especially evident in the Biblical accounts of the raising of the dead by Jesus. In the case of the daughter of Jairus, who had just departed this life, Jesus (according to Luke 8:54) simply says: "Maid, arise;" with the young man of Nain, who is about to be buried, He becomes more urgent: "Young man, I say unto thee, Arise" (Luke 7:14). Finally, in the case of Lazarus, who had already been lying in the grave for four days, Jesus prays, before crying with a loud voice: "Lazarus, come forth" (John 11:41-43).

In this connection I must yet refer to something that is extremely important for us all to know and heed, namely that again and again it happens that close relatives break out into loud lamenting in a death chamber, and try to make the departing one say something further. However understandable this may be from their standpoint, they are unknowingly guilty of a gross lack of consideration for the dying person, for the wish is thus awakened in him still to be able to make himself understood in an earthly way by means of the physical body from which he was just about to sever himself. His wish now runs counter to this process, for through it, he seeks to bind himself again to the earthly. This leads to a renewed densification of the connection-cord, which thereby again becomes more adapted to being a channel for pain. Through such a longing, the dying person is thus more firmly bound to the physical body again, and compelled to feel its pains once more. This results in an unintended prolonging of the process of dying, in a death struggle sometimes dragging on for days, because the personal volition of the dying one has interfered with the process. Therefore absolute quiet should reign in a chamber of death, a dignified solemnity in keeping with the important hour.

I believe that no serious-minded person who has grasped what takes place at death can evade the logic of this. For death is nothing but rebirth into a world beyond, from which we came. Let us therefore strive not to make this step hard, particularly for a loved one, through our grief, which in reality is selfishness.

Now after hearing all this it will be easy for us to understand the experiences of the persons questioned by Dr. Moody. Since we have also dealt with the subject of sleep, we can undertake to classify these experiences, for they are always to be found in the realm between sleep and death. There are accounts of people who lay seriously ill and who on the threshold between life and death saw deceased relatives or helpers from the beyond, and spoke with them. Then finally there are the descriptions of those who found themselves already outside their bodies, and of those who already had been considered "clinically dead." But none of these was really dead, that is, the connection-cord had not yet been severed. It is just through this that these descriptions of intermediate stages on the way from life to death complement the picture of that smooth transition of which I have already spoken. The nightly dream-images still partly superimposed by the impressions of the day, the visions of the beyond by the dangerously ill, the withdrawal of the physical body with the subsequent ever further-reaching experiences of the presumed death, and finally death, all appear as though arranged in sequence.

Therefore, Dr. Moody has rightly arrived at the conclusion, "In general persons who were 'dead' seem to report more lasting, complete experiences than those who only came close to death, and those who were 'dead' for a longer period go deeper than those who were 'dead' for a short time." This implies that the further the loosening of the soul has progressed, and its consequent withdrawal from the physical body, the more impressions of the beyond it experiences.

Thus the perceiving of persons who were invisible to others— hence those visions the dangerously ill experienced—is still very close to the experiencing in the beyond of people who are dreaming. The body-radiation of the seriously ill, however, is already so much diminished that the soul is able to loosen itself even a little more than during dreaming. Therefore, it already sees the world of the beyond more clearly, more distinctly, no longer mingled with daytime impressions absorbed by the brain, as is frequently the case with our dreams.

The next perplexing new experience is that of the "out of the body state," of no longer being in the body. Here the soul, no longer held fast enough by the body-radiation, has already drawn the astral body away from the physical body, and the real man, the spirit, now looks through this astral body at the physical body. In this state, people were able to see what was happening around their physical bodies, they heard the words of those standing by, they could even recognize their thoughts just before they were uttered. But how is this possible?

Here too it is a matter of something completely natural. Just as our gross material physical body possesses the sense-organs corresponding to its consistency, so also the astral body and the ethereal body are similarly equipped. But it is always our spirit that sees, hears or feels through the sense-organs of the particular outermost covering, thus never the eye or the ear itself. The spirit within the astral body thus perceives through the sense-organs of the latter.

We must become fundamentally clear as to the real nature of these worlds in the beyond that already begin with the astral plane, and especially about what makes them different from our world. I have said that our earthly world is only a solidification arising from radiation. "Solidification" implies loss of lightness and mobility; it means becoming more sluggish or heavier. With any earthly substance that melts, vaporizes, and becomes gaseous, we can observe this as an opposite process. Its dematerialization and increasing lightness are based on an ever faster movement of its atoms. In other words, ultimately, finer, lighter forms are only ever-faster states of movement. Now please think of a radio receiver. It comprises different wave-bands: medium waves, short waves, ultra-short waves. If you switch from one band to the other, the set is suddenly able to receive higher frequencies, thus livelier vibrations, which until then were not accessible to it. The reason for this is that it is now tuned in, that is, its receiving equipment is homogeneous with these oscillations and can therefore receive them. Thus, we too bear within us different "receiving and transmitting equipment" for different wave-bands in the form of the physical body, the astral body and the soul body. For this reason the "out of the body state" involves first a "switch over" to the immediately adjoining wave-band of a higher frequency. The division here is not so sharp as in a radio-receiver; the transitions are again smooth. Since the astral sphere is still very near to the earthly, the departing one, who gradually begins to change over to the "frequency band" of the other world is at first still able to include both sides in his perceptions. Thus he can recognize the thoughts whose vibrations lie within this range when they have become so concentrated that they are just about to be uttered. At the same time, he can still see and hear the earthly.

However, he can no longer make himself perceptible. If you have followed the explanations so far, it will be clear that it simply cannot be otherwise. The instrument for earthly communication is the earthly body, from which by this time the dying person has already departed and which at this stage he can no longer move. Even the astral body-covering is generally invisible to our gross material eyes; the words he forms with it remain in a sphere of radiation to which our sense-organs are just as unreceptive as they are to the radio or television waves constantly surrounding us. Nor does our earthly body respond to the touch of the astral or even the ethereal body of the departed. This state of being no longer heard, no longer seen, is a painfully distressing experience for one who passes over without knowing about these processes. He sees his relatives mourning and would like to call out to them, "What is the matter with you? I am still alive!" He sees the doctors handling his body and would like to drive them away, but no one takes any notice of him. The ignorant person feels himself to be alive in the intermediate region and yet expelled from all the living. It is an experience of terrifying loneliness.

May you recognize from this how senseless it is to have pushed aside everything connected with dying as though just the most inevitable thing in this earth-life had nothing at all to do with us.

Even now, when people are at last prepared to break the taboo, they are caught at the boundary of what they believe can still be "scientifically" proved. What matters is to enlighten people unreservedly about everything associated with death and what takes place at that time, because all this belongs inseparably to the great oneness of our existence. We shall all have to cross this threshold one day. Is it not better to do so knowingly, instead of being pushed into the unknown?

Such knowledge is essential for us not only for this hour, which is approaching every one of us, but already beforehand. Thus, at funerals people follow a coffin. How few of the so-called mourners remember the deceased with loving thoughts! How much evil or trivial talk often goes on in a funeral procession. If these people knew that the deceased is perhaps still near, that he can hear them, they would behave differently.

Let us return to Dr. Moody's report on "Life after Life." Many of the persons questioned by him had indeed experienced more than the "out of the body state." Where they "had penetrated more deeply into the realm of death" they had a remarkable experience. They felt as if they were gliding through something dark and narrow—a valley, a dark shaft, a tunnel. Difficult as it is to put an experience in the beyond into earthly words, those concerned characteristically agreed in speaking of being "pulled out" of, or on their return being "drawn in" to, earth-life. Here, we are therefore dealing with the next phase, the striving away of the ethereal soul from the astral body, thus the soul's pulling out from the latter. At these moments of transition, of the striving away, the spirit can now no longer see through the eyes of the earthly or astral body, nor yet through those of the ethereal body, which is only about to become free. Therefore, the spirit temporarily has the impression of darkness. It is as though one were inside an elevator moving between two floors. There we cannot look out either, but must wait until the next floor is reached.

This next stage that the soul now enters is a world of faster vibrations, and is emphasized by an acoustic experience that the persons questioned had while being "pulled out." They heard a noise, and described it as the booming of a bell, a rushing, a roaring, a bang. Thereafter they found themselves suddenly in the brightness of a new world, the earthly had disappeared from them. For the soul, the entry into its new form of existence is like the breaking of a sound barrier. It changes over into a world of faster vibration.

Another result of this faster vibration is the change in the concept of time. Here too, we see the fundamental relationship between dream and death. Already in dreams the wealth of what has been experienced often does not coincide with the earthly time that has elapsed; we think we have been dreaming for much longer. One of those questioned by Dr. Moody summarized the experience in the beyond, which went even further in this respect, in the sentence, "As soon as one has detached oneself from the earthly body, everything seems to speed up." This too, is self-evident and simply could not be otherwise. Owing to its faster intrinsic movement the ethereal soul-body is lighter, thus more permeable, and this brings with it an increased receptivity to experiencing. Everything that happens affects the spirit much more directly through the less dense covering. It is able at the same time to grasp, that is, to experience, much more than we can, because every happening can move the spirit much more directly. Here it is fundamentally a question of the same Law that we can also observe in the earthly: the more different electromagnetic frequencies a cable can transport, the more conversations we can simultaneously transmit along it; the higher the frequency of the light with which we take a photograph, the more detail it will show us, so long as the frequency is matched to that of the object being photographed. In this increased ability to comprehend, which is characteristic of faster movement, is found an easily verifiable explanation, based on the Laws of Nature, of the apparently so enigmatic saying "a thousand years are as one day."

However, the altered feeling of time in the world beyond shows us very clearly that, regarding the concept of time, we are under a misapprehension. We generally understand it by minutes, hours, days and years. Yet these are only a measure, derived from the movement of the earth about the sun. We all know that one hour does not equal another, that an hour of joy seems short to us, while one of pain seems like an eternity.

Rich experiencing makes time pass as if on wings, while during inactive waiting it crawls by. Time is not the hour or the date, but the abundance of what we are able to experience, to accumulate in it. Hugo von Hofmannsthal expressed this very well when he said, "To the one who experiences, life expands." That is why it is so significant that, through the experience in the beyond of those who had briefly departed this life, this recognition is called to our consciousness and deepened. It already means the first step toward answering the ever-repeated question about the purpose of our life. We realize that to live means to experience!

In this connection another experience, which those who hovered between life and death were able to have, gains special significance. They experienced that in the world beyond a completely different kind of knowledge counts. It was, as they described it, a deeper knowledge, a knowing as it were "with the soul," which is connected with the origins and interweavings of that which "holds the world together at its core." To acquire this kind of knowledge, as they were told by helpful beings in the beyond, is the most important thing, even here on earth. This should not only make us think, but also arouse us. For it shows how wrong our education is, how much precious time in our life we spend on learning things which, after all, are quite unimportant. Here runs the dividing line between the intellect and the spirit. What we acquire by learning is of use to the intellect; stored in the cells of our brain it remains behind with our physical body. Only what we experience, perceive intuitively, what moves our spirit, enters into us; that alone can we take with us. But today the whole of mankind suffers from a one-sided intellectual development. We accomplish splendid works of technology, but we lack the ability to control them, to use them wisely, because instead of letting ourselves be guided by the spirit, we have left the guidance to the spirit's earthly instrument, the intellect. Thus we interfere everywhere in natural happenings, without being able to foresee the consequences, because we lack the true knowledge of the structure of this Creation. The deeply moving recognition of Goethe's *Faust* has unfortunately lost none of its validity even today: "Oh happy he who can still hope to rise out of this flood of errors! What we do not know is just what we need to know, and what we know we cannot make use of!"

All who during the temporary withdrawal from their physical body had left the earthly world, experienced the nearness of a loving light-being, who mediated to them a review of their earth-life. Entirely of themselves, they came to recognize how much had been wrong in it, how much suffering they had caused others, often unknowingly, and how much time they had wasted. Some of them returned to earthly life with the greatest reluctance and even remonstrated vehemently with their rescuers. All who had been "over there" brought back with them the resolve to live differently, more consciously, in the future.

I consider this to be really the most important of what these reports about life after death have given us. This review of life, the insight and the conclusions drawn from it, are surely the clear sign of a responsibility of which the spirit immediately becomes conscious as soon as it has laid aside the shackles of the earthly, for then its intellectual considerations of earthly expediency, its doubts, have been removed automatically. However, responsibility can never be an end in itself. It can only grow in connection with a task. Thus man has a task, but who is to tell us what it is?

It is just at this decisive point that we are let down by parapsychology and thanatology, and by those books and writings that deal with life before this life and life after our death. Together they can tell us nothing more than this: earth-life is a passage in a further-reaching existence, and above all, death is not the end.

That in itself is extremely important. You have already heard how the mere knowledge of a continued life can one day make severance from the earthly body much easier. Yet the importance of this knowledge goes even further. Once you have pushed open the gate to the wholeness of your existence, your gaze will reach beyond this earth-life. You will not then feel yourself totally bound up with the earthly, like those who bind themselves to it, of their own accord, through the belief that they would live only here and only once. Such an attitude in a human being brings forth its consequences at the time of death. Through this clinging to the earth the ethereal soul-body also becomes denser and thus heavier because its wishes, directed toward the earth, need to be as close to the earth as possible. With this I am already going beyond what is contained in the reports compiled by Dr. Moody. But let us not forget that all these people were not actually dead. They had only temporarily left their earthly body for greater or lesser distances. When they gave an account of it they had already come back into this body, though some of them may have died later. At the time when they had the experiences described, the ethereal connection-cord of which I spoke earlier was not yet severed. All these descriptions therefore relate to an intermediate realm, a short-term transition. They do indeed confirm to us the existence of a "beyond," and of an extraterrestrial life, but they tell us nothing about what happens to the soul after final severance from the earthly body, thus after the disintegration of the "silver cord."

Here, in the interest of completing my explanations, I must still take this important next step, for all too easily the erroneous impression could otherwise arise that the beyond had only joyful things to offer everyone. The fate of the ethereal soul after the final severance depends, of course, on the lightness or heaviness of the ethereal body. We create its variation for ourselves through the aims we give to our desires. The higher they are, in the rightly understood spiritual sense, the lighter will our soul-body become, and the more base they are the denser it will become. Indeed we experience within us that gloomy thoughts "weigh us down," earthly worries "burden" us, make our heart "heavy," but a noble intuitive perception, a serene disposition, "uplifts" us, makes us "winged," and we feel "light at heart." These descriptions are no empty illusion. They are the absolutely fitting description of a process in which the ethereal body participates very decisively, because every such stirring of our spirit, the intuitive perception, can only manifest in the earthly body by way of the ethereal body.

The moment the cord that binds us here to our earthly body has disintegrated, this ethereal "soul" rises or falls according to the Law of Gravity familiar to us all. We know this law as buoyancy (in water it is called "Archimedes' Principle"), but it manifests most clearly with gases. Any earthly substance, when it changes into a gaseous state, thus when it has become finer and lighter, takes its place according to the Law of Gravity. Through this law, heaven and hell are also explained, because it causes a completely natural separation. At the place to which the Law of Gravity automatically leads it, every soul will be surrounded by such souls as have the same weight, and therefore essentially the same nature. This being together with their kind may be heaven for some, but for others, as long as they themselves do not bring about a change through a judicious transformation of their volition, it may be hell.

28

Once we have grasped that after the falling away of the physical body our place is determined by the Law of Gravity, which automatically separates the homogeneous species at any given time, we shall have come another major step nearer the answer to the question of the meaning of our life. We will then recognize that this, our earthly body, is a mantle, a protective wall, which like a diving-bell through its weight, holds us fast in the gross material substance of this earth-world, making it possible for human beings of the most diverse character to live together side by side. Hence the Earth is a reservoir, a meeting-point for what otherwise would have to remain separate. I will speak about the significance of this fact later.

Thus you see that to become clear about death really means first to occupy oneself rightly with life. Dag Hammerskjöld, the late Secretary-General of the United Nations, expressed this very aptly. He said, "If we go to the root of the matter, it is our concept of death that decides our answers to all the questions which life poses."

But does not this very statement reveal the helplessness of even those who think seriously? Though we may know that this life is only harnessed between the poles of the before and the after, nevertheless we are living here and now, and here and now we need to be clear about where to find the answers to the questions of life.

Now you may ask, what is the purpose of religions? On the part of their bringers, the teachings were originally meant to be a support to us, and lead to the truth they held in common. However, since from the very beginning they were not passed on in written form, misunderstandings have entered into them. The personal understanding of those who transmitted the teachings has altered something in them, narrowed them down. In the course of centuries the content was eventually adapted more and more to human wishes, and the picture was arranged as we would like to see it. I would like to remind you that the so decisively important doctrine of reincarnation, of rebirth as a human being, through which the Love and Justice of God first became intelligible to human spirits, was only expunged from Christian creeds at the Council of Constantinople in the year 553, for purely political reasons, in accordance with the wishes of Emperor Justinian I.

And now please reflect that if at that time Emperor Justinian had decided differently, reincarnation would be a matter of course for Western humanity. There would then be no need to contend with walls of doubt and of prejudice, to free our thinking from that dreadful constraint into which it has fallen solely through this unhappy decision that has robbed us of the outlook on the connections and the vastness of our existence. So you see that man has presumed to decide what is allowed to be true! This has caused the inconsistencies and gaps that prevent so many thinking people from accepting fully the tenets of faith. But Truth must convince in its entirety; there can be no reservations about it.

What is left for us of all the wise teachings are admonitions and rules of conduct. Most of these are of high moral value, but they lack the cohesion that could form a world-picture able to give us the answer to those questions that simply cannot be evaded. They are first of all the question of the purpose of our existence, and secondly, the question of how we can fulfill such a purpose.

You may smile, and think to yourself, "Is that all?" I am fully aware that throughout time the most eminent thinkers have racked their brains about this. But what has come of it? In many cases, only conflicting philosophical dogmas aimed at proving the intellectual sophistry of their founding fathers, rather than giving genuine vital help. Yet I dare to assert that the answers are not so difficult to find, nor are they so intricate and complicated as they appear to us, for all Truth is simple. It is just in simplicity, which is a result of the uniformity of the whole, that true greatness lies. We do know today, to mention only a few examples, that the immense variety of plants, animals, and human beings has its foundation in the same four genetic building-stones, that the cells in plant, animal, and man are built up in the same way; that every cell, in whatever organ it may be located, always contains the master-plan of the whole. We know that arms, legs, wings, and fins have issued from the same fundamental design. We know that the same forces with similar characteristics are at work within an atom as between the solar systems. Does this not teach us that everything is based on uniform laws, that only the variation in their effects causes the multiplicity that seems confusing to us?

What we need therefore is an overall perspective. Hence, I must again speak of *In the Light of Truth: The Grail Message.* It would lead too far if we were to enter here into the significance of the Holy Grail. Our mental image of it is linked with the concept of something sublime, sacred. May this suffice to allow us to perceive the origin of that helpful Call sent to mankind in *The Grail Message,* and to convey a faint idea of the loftiness of this view, which lies incomparably far above all that is offered us in other descriptions of the beyond. Therefore, the Author could say:

"*I wish to fill the gaps which have hitherto remained unanswered in the souls of men, and which will never leave a serious thinker in peace if he is honestly seeking for the Truth.*"

I have used a few points of what is stated in *The Grail Message* as the basis for the explanation about the nature of death and the process of dying, but this Message contains and tells us much more. It not only takes from us the fear of death, it takes from us something much more important: the fear of life. If you were to study this work you would experience the rightness

31

of the sentence, the significance of which simply cannot be fathomed, which summarizes its content and states:

"*With my Message I now open the Book of Creation for you!*"

As you will surely understand, I cannot in the course of a single lecture unfold before you a world-picture of such immense breadth, which also shows our path in this Creation. I must continue to confine myself to what is most important. It seems to me, as already mentioned, that this most important factor is the question of the purpose of our life. On this account so many human beings despair, since they can find no answer. They escape into excesses, into the sham world of drugs, throw themselves into the arms of the false teachings of religious impostors, or thoughtlessly endanger this life, which to them appears meaningless and therefore worthless. Indeed, they even throw it away.

Does not even a glance into this Creation tell us that everything in it has a purpose? Ecology, the science of natural cooperation, reveals to us how one thing fits into another, completing and furthering each other. In this interplay of the great household of Creation, everything fulfills the role assigned to it. How then could we assume that man alone is without function in this system?

Every search for the purpose of life, however, if it does not reach purely nihilistic conclusions, is in danger of dealing only with abstract ideas. We do not want to lose our foothold, nor is this at all necessary, for even what is greatest is always reflected in the small, and everything in which lies the great Truth of this Creation can be found portrayed in the world around us. You will surely have already noticed that I have referred again and again to experiences familiar to us all, or to

32

recognitions of the natural sciences. I do so in order that you may learn that the processes just described run their courses exactly according to the same Laws.

I said earlier that the core of man, his real ego, is spirit. Now in that part of the text that I have brought to your attention to clarify this concept, it was said that the spiritual world lies higher and forms the upper, lightest part of Creation. So what are we, as spiritual creatures, doing here in the earthly?

The inadequacy of our institutions, of our human activity, already bears the answer within it. Man is not a fully developed spirit. His spirit-core is a seed-grain, a spiritual germ. Like every seed-grain, it contains the full potentialities of its species, but it must ripen gradually.

What does Nature do to enable the seed of a plant to ripen? It is rooted into the earth. The manifold forces thereby working on it advance and strengthen it.

Now consider that the Creator has done likewise with us. We are sunk into this earthly world as seed-grains. Only the species distinguishes us from the ripening of the plant. We are in the World of Matter for the maturing of our own species, the spirit. The earthly experiencing with its constant need to overcome difficulties caused by material substance—just think for instance of the proverb, "the spirit is willing, but the flesh is weak"—is meant to help us recognize the power of the spirit within us, and to strengthen it for conscious activity. How significant it is, in view of the fundamental uniformity of the Laws of Nature, that even physically we need friction with material substance to move step by step, to progress. And only here, in the mantle of this dense-material corporeality, is it also possible, as I have said earlier, for human beings of different levels of spiritual maturity to be able to live together on the same plane. This, however, offers us a diversity of experience not possible in other spheres. It is this diversity of experience that facilitates the ability to mature, and makes earth-life so important.

Where is this development ultimately to lead us? The answer is supplied by our nature: it leads to the Spiritual Realm that corresponds to our species, but which we can only attain in a fully matured state.

Consider, please, the structure of Creation. Let us begin right away with ourselves. The organelles in every cell are independent industries, but at the same time part of the wholeness of the cell, which in turn is part of the tissues. The tissues form organs, which in their turn are parts of groups of organs. These finally make up the body. A single human being is an independent creature, and yet part of the family; this is part of a group that by way of the village, the people, and the race, finally embraces the whole of mankind. Everything is embedded in these hierarchical gradations, which in the material world reach from elementary particles to atoms and molecules, right up to celestial bodies, solar systems, and galaxies.

Within this structure we find everywhere the dual function of all that exists, namely to be an independent whole and also part of a greater order. This involves two apparently conflicting necessities: self-assertion of the individual whole, and at the same time its fitting into, integrating, with a greater unit. In this connection I would like to quote to you from the recent book by scientist-philosopher Arthur Koestler (*Der Mensch: Irrläufer der Evolution*, Scherz-Verlag, Bern/Munich): "The constellation Self-assertion versus Integration . . . exists in biology, psychology, ecology, and wherever we encounter complex hierarchical systems, thus practically everywhere we look. In the living animal or the living plant each part must assert its individuality just as in the social system, because otherwise the organism would lose its structure and disintegrate.

But at the same time each part must bow to the demand of the whole. In a healthy organism and a healthy society the two tendencies are balanced at all levels of the hierarchy."

Herein lies the confirmation of what is shown to us in *The Grail Message*. Just as it is for everything earthly, so it applies to us also at every stage of our spiritual development, with the spiritual abilities we have so far developed, to integrate ourselves as personalities into the community. Quite a few people believe that the final goal of our path is Nirvana, the complete dissolution of our ego into an all-embracing power. The mistaken idea that the ego is something deserving of destruction could only arise because here, on this low earthly plane, we know it for the most part only as selfishness, as egotism. Koestler says the following on this point: "In a healthy organism and a healthy society the two tendencies are balanced at all levels of the hierarchy." Therefore, let us not derive the task assigned to us in the order of Creation from the faulty current state, but from the healthy desired state. From this it follows that the goal of our existence can lie only in cooperating with the mechanism of this Creation as a fully matured spirit, while remaining personal. The more conscious we become in achieving this goal, the easier, of course, it comes to us to fit in, since we recognize increasingly that this order of Creation is so perfect that cooperating in service within it means, at the same time, the greatest personal advantage. Out of a free volition, we are then prepared to help in the realization of the great order, because it holds happiness for us personally.

If for once we fully grasp this inwardly, it must become clear to us that there can be nothing more beautiful for the human spirit than voluntary service. For "voluntary" means unhindered by ties, which must be discussed later. It means being allowed to follow one's own volition, thus to act out of innermost conviction. This freedom of will alone releases the concept of serving from its association of slavish subjection to an alien will, releases it also from the appearance of spiritual passivity. It is a joyfully active, conscious serving, being of use to a more comprehensive purpose beyond our own person. This longing to be of use lies deeply rooted in each one of us. Is it not the worst thing for the unemployed, for the old, to see no task before them, to be needed no longer? This indeed reveals how much our spirit longs to fulfill its mission!

The matured homecoming to the source of our species, to the high luminous World of the Spirit, is thus the individually personal goal that is set for each one of us. But at the same time, there follows from this at every level the task for the community. Man, equipped with the core of a higher species imbued with the urge to develop, is here already enabled and called to be the connecting-link between the material world and the Spiritual Realm. He is meant to form the bridge by which, uplifting and ennobling, the beauty and harmony of that higher world flows down into the earthly. True art, which outlives the ages, is an example of the fulfillment of this task.

Is it not remarkable that, undeterred by all baseness, disregarding all the dreadful things that man has done in the course of his history and still does to his fellow man, the concept of humanity for us is nevertheless still associated with the idea of love for our neighbor, dignity and noble-mindedness? This embryonically-traced image of the higher purpose of man's existence, towards which he has to develop, is indestructibly imprinted on the human spirit.

Now we have found the answer to the question of the purpose of our life, but it still remains for us to clarify how we can achieve its realization.

Here in truth lies our human problem: we know little of that great order that must become joyfully self-evident to us. The guilt for this lies with us. Creation itself is the language in which the Creator speaks to us. Just as a child must learn the language of his parents to know what is expected of him, and what he must do, so man has to strive to understand the language of Creation. Therefore, the Author of *The Grail Message* calls to us:

"*Learn to understand Creation aright in its Laws! Therein lies the way upwards to the Light!*"

Just looking up at the starry skies teaches us that the planets trace their courses in accordance with unchangeable Laws, and only because of this may we calculate planetary courses. Here, in the Laws which order and uphold all that exists, and which indeed surround us here on all sides, we meet with the infallible support that we must find lacking everywhere else. How then could we still doubt the rightness of the sentence contained in *The Grail Message*:

> "*The man who knows Creation in its lawful activity will soon understand the sublime Will of God in it also.*"

To recognize this Will of God is indispensable for us. But is it not strange that in our criminal code we have established ignorance of the law as being no protection from punishment? That is to say, he who transgresses the existing norms has to take the consequences in any case. It is his fault if he has not troubled to acquaint himself with the laws.

To mention only one example, even if we authorize someone to drive a motor vehicle we require him to pass a test to prove his knowledge of the relevant laws, because, in our opinion, he would otherwise be a danger to himself and others.

How sensible, how judicious we are in these matters! Does it not occur to us then that the Creator too might be as wise as we are, and that the same principle might apply also to us regarding the Laws of this Creation?

But how have we acted until now? We have left it to the scientists to concern themselves with these Laws, because we have regarded them as Laws of Nature. At best they have interested us only insofar as we could make use of them technically. But we have neglected to draw lessons from them for ourselves as spiritual creatures. The physicist, Walter Heitler, Professor at the University of Zurich (*Man and Science*, Oliver and Boyd, 1963), is of the same opinion: "But the time is indeed ripe for us to begin to be aware of the metaphysical questions concealed behind the Laws of Nature."

Our knowledge has doubled in the last three decades alone. Specialist fields are beginning to merge and a great unity is becoming apparent. Here and there already we find the beginnings of a concept of wholeness. More and more we recognize the rightness of the sentence long since written in *The Grail Message*:

"*Indeed everything in Creation works reciprocally.*"

Even scientists now speak of an "intermeshed" world. We can no longer act as though this network had nothing to do with us. We are interwoven with it, not only bodily-physically but also in our human-spiritual existence, because the continuous validity of all the Laws of Creation does not stop short of us. Only the consequences of these Laws affect at one time the earthly, then the ethereal or the spiritual, according to the species concerned. We have even known of this uniformity for a long time; we have only forgotten it. You must all be familiar with the well-known words of truth: as you sow, so shall you reap; you have made your bed: now lie in it; take heed or take the consequences. These statements are nothing but the abbreviations of experiences that man has had with the Law of Reciprocal Action, one of the most important and fundamental Laws of Creation. No one would dispute that the metaphors used also contain a figurative meaning, thus that material and spiritual happenings have here been quite consciously equated.

Only a few decades ago it was recognized that this lawfulness even has a much more far-reaching significance. In it lies also a self-regulating factor that ultimately provides for the maintenance of an unchangeable order.

Norbert Wiener, who was the first to make possible the technical application of this principle, coined for it the term cybernetics, derived from the Greek word "kybernetes," which means much the same as "helmsman." It was clear to him that in the machines he invented, the computers, he was reproducing modes of action that are characteristic of living creatures. He therefore also called his book *Cybernetics, or the Transfer of Information in Living Creatures and Machines.* However, he had not considered that everything that takes place in living creatures is simply a lawfulness of what is living. What could be more living than this Creation as a whole, which from the greatest to the smallest is full of ceaseless movement? Thus it was gradually realized that these automatic regulating-processes are to be found everywhere, that they are inherent not only throughout the household of Nature, but inevitably also in human institutions. They even determine historical and economic processes, social structures, sports, languages, the judicial system and inter-human relationships. In short, there is nothing that could not be traced back to the workings of this automatic regulating, quite simply because everything has issued from the vitality of this Creation, and through it alone can continue to exist. Thus we have before us a fundamental Law of the whole mechanism of Creation, and with it an excellent opportunity of illustrating what it means to get to know Creation in its Laws. You will see how many fundamental questions are answered in them.

We make use of cybernetic lawfulness in all kinds of automatic devices and computers, without which our present way of life can hardly be imagined. Thus you need not be a technician to understand the governing principle present in it. For instance, whether you preset the desired temperature on your refrigerator or central heating, select a certain program for your washing-machine, or dishwasher, or whether an electronic brain combines a mass of data to maintain a pre-arranged objective, it is only a question of the order of magnitude, but not of the principle. You are surely aware that such equipment has to be "programmed." Here, too, the essence of the principle consists in absolute and optimum realization of this "program," in that all influences interfering with the course of the program release an automatic reaction, which in turn eliminates the interference.

Now, ladies and gentlemen, let us apply this principle, which as stated can be encountered in all kinds of processes, and which has only been technically imitated by us, to the whole of Creation. Do not the Natural Laws, which we only can discover and take note of but not change, then appear to us as the "program" according to which everything that takes place in the mechanism of Creation runs its course? But from where does this program come? Surely it does not arise of itself; as we know, there must be a "programmer." Must not the Creator then appear to us as the One who drew up this program and fed it into Creation? You see, when a person programs a computer he does so according to his will, that is he feeds his will into it in the form of the "program." The world-mechanism operating according to the same Laws of automatic control therefore bears within it the Will of God; it is *His* Will that appears to us as Natural Law.

Please bear in mind at this point that it is part of the essence of automatic control-mechanisms to guarantee the best possible end result. If we succeed in doing so with a computer, must we not then, applying it to the great picture, all the more conclude that this was possible also for the Creator? Likewise must we not conclude that the Laws of Creation or of Nature provide for the best that is possible? But this opens up to us an entirely new, immense focal point, for the best, the optimal, is of course the highest attainable, and thus perfection. In these Laws of Nature therefore the Perfection of God reveals itself. This also explains their immovability, for what is perfect cannot be improved; any change could only be for the worse. Therefore, wherever we try to correct this perfection we experience setbacks.

But does this not also show us how wrong our picture of God has been? There is no room for the concept of the old gentleman who would allow himself to be moved by our pleading and begging to dispense leniency or favor. The picture of Him that this world unmistakably holds out is incomparably greater, more powerful and sublime than we could ever conceive. God's omnipotence, therefore, does not consist in arbitrary proceedings that we associate with the idea of power; it is the all-embracing Power, which in the long run, because of its immovable perfection, nothing can resist.

This Creation-wide basic Law of automatic control, which seeks to eliminate every disturbance, also explains the concept of fate. It is the balancing reaction to that which we ourselves have brought into being. Here too, we see that ignorance of the Laws does not protect us from the consequences, but insight into the error comes to us more easily if we have not committed it consciously. We need not confine ourselves to the abstract in these considerations, for we find examples of this in all natural happenings. If for instance you decide to run a 100-meter race, you cannot prevent yourself from panting when you have reached the goal. Through the exertion of running you have reduced the optimum supply of air for your physical body, and now this automatically enforces the balance. You only need to alter the scale of this example within the framework of the Creation-wide Laws of control to find the answer to the question of man's free will and his fate. As these control-Laws demonstrate to us, we are indeed free to make decisions, but we are bound to their consequences. Nevertheless, in the course of our existence—here I am deliberately not speaking only of this earth-life—we have already made countless decisions, whose consequences do not always come about as instantaneously as in the example quoted earlier. We often find ourselves bound, constrained by the inescapable pressure of such reactions. We then doubt the freedom of will, and speak of dependence, of fate. But what appears to us as fate, because of its inevitability, is nothing other than the reaction of our own intuitive perception, thought and deed, which is "sent" to us to make up for what we confused and entangled in the great order of Creation. Similarly, with a piece of string you can untie a knot only by pulling it back through the loop through which it was formed. Therefore, suicide is never a way out of existing difficulties either, for it does not exempt the one concerned from the need to undo the self-made knot. Rather, it burdens him with the additional guilt of having disregarded the gift of being allowed to mature. The injustice, which seems like punishment to us, has ultimately a much wider meaning: it is an appeal to our reason, with the aim of leading us back upon the only right path, which to our detriment, we were about to forsake. Thus, it is a matter of a solicitous nudge to correct our course. In this reciprocal action, which brings to each what he himself has released, lies inseparably united the Justice and the Love of God. He has done His part from the very beginning, by placing His Will, which also provides what is best for us, in this Creation as Law. It is up to us at last to make the most of the opportunities thereby granted us, for **in them** lies God's ever-present Grace, which we have only to grasp.

It is not only this immovable, automatic working of the Laws of Creation, the ever-ready help for us within them, but also the necessities arising from them, which *In the Light of Truth: The Grail Message* describes and explains. The discovery of automatic control techniques, of cybernetics, has confirmed the rightness of these explanations, and thus also the significance of the following sentence from *The Grail Message*:

"O nly the man who lives in the Laws of God is free!"

The reasoning has now become understandable to us. Only such a man, as the automatic Law of Reciprocal Action teaches us, can avoid painful reactions that restrict his freedom of will, and partake fully of the help that lies in the Laws of God.

Therefore, also Jesus, who from His origin was Himself a part of the Truth contained in these immovable Laws, was able to say not only, "I am . . . the Truth and the Life," but also, "He that is not with me is against me," since everything that does not fit in with these Laws disturbs the continuous "running of the program" of this Creation.

Therefore, these Laws also permit us to recognize that we may not continue indefinitely being unthinking disturbers of the great harmony of Creation. Ecological processes, which of course take place in accordance with the same Laws, demonstrate clearly that a wrong development once begun accelerates increasingly, finally approaching a point where a catastrophe is unavoidable. Some years ago, leading scientists hinted at this in their report to the "Club of Rome."

And how are things done in our educational systems? We allow a pupil who has not achieved the required standard to repeat examinations, even to repeat the class. One day, however, there comes an end to these opportunities for someone who does not know how to make use of them. The goal set must be reached within a definite time. Were it not so it would only mean the encouragement of laziness and an unwillingness to learn. Let us not consider the Creator as less wise than ourselves, who can only imitate what already exists in Creation! We too are given the opportunity, through reincarnation and rebirth, to make up for the mistakes we have made in the Material World, and which therefore also have to be redeemed here. That we are unable to remember earlier lives with our day consciousness—I mention this only in passing—is not at all important. For the day-conscious recollection is formed through the storage of proteins in our brain. But this brain disintegrates with physical death. What we have experienced, however, what has formed us, has become part of our spirit; it constitutes our inclinations, our abilities, in short our personality, with which we enter into a new life, or better expressed, continue our existence. But—and I will return after this short digression to what I said earlier—everything points to the fact that we do not have unlimited time for judicious learning. Viewed thus, it appears significant that the meeting of the "Club of Rome," which took place in June 1979 in Salzburg, was concerned with the need to study the Creation-wide connections without which the continued existence of humanity would seem to be in jeopardy. With this an immense circle closes, the beyond and this world unite for the same appeal. This admonition was given also to those who had already briefly glimpsed the beyond, and it coincides with the words already quoted from *The Grail Message*:

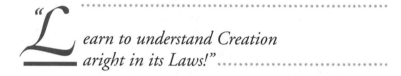

"*Learn to understand Creation aright in its Laws!*"

These Laws are not a sophisticated system of thought such as theology and philosophy offer us, but immovable, indisputable living reality. Through them, and only through them, can that which, with cryptic ambiguity, is generally called "belief" become conviction for us, because this belief is confirmed daily through the Laws of this Creation. Thus we find also, as the first sentence in *The Grail Message*, the words that hold out to every seeker the best that can happen to him:

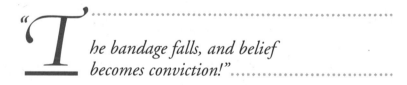

"*The bandage falls, and belief becomes conviction!*"

This is a completely new note in matters of belief, a note to which our ear should be particularly receptive just at this time, when the confusion caused by our lack of understanding is everywhere recoiling upon us, for how else could we still find the way out?

To many people this automatic irrevocability of the Laws may seem hard, even frightening, because, in our own interest, they are demanding. Do we not all know the proverbial words of wisdom: "The mills of God grind slowly, yet they grind exceedingly fine?"

What is described here as "the mills of God" is surely nothing other than the natural Law of Reciprocal Action, and the certain arrival of the reciprocal action testifies to its irrevocability. The discovery of the technique of automatic control and its application to the whole of Creation therefore only confirm in modern technical guise an ancient empirical knowledge. It tells us that this application likewise to extra-material happenings is not only permissible, but also right.

This fundamentally loving severity is at the same time also a criterion for the seriousness with which you yourself approach these questions. Here it is a matter of deciding whether you wish to form God according to your image, or to pay attention to His Will. The Author of *The Grail Message* has therefore written even in his preface:

"*I* am addressing earnest seekers only."

I may assume such earnestness on the part of you who have followed my explanations concerning fundamental questions of our existence.

I can well imagine that you still have many questions. During this lecture I could only discuss very little. *In the Light of Truth: The Grail Message* presents the answers far better than I could. It is a work—I would like emphatically to stress this, because I have been repeatedly asked about it—which, in spite of its alleged similarity with the basic truths of other teachings, cannot be coordinated with any of these, even from the mere fact that the explanation of the relationships given in it reaches incomparably further. Therefore, do not imagine that you could begin anywhere, because you perhaps think that you have already heard this or that. There is a structure in the book that imperceptibly, but from the very beginning, leads you into a new kind of seeing and experiencing. You will perhaps ask yourself why I consistently refer to *The Grail Message*. I will tell you quite frankly the reason, for you are not to think you have come to a propaganda meeting. Again and again I experience, in private as well as in my profession as a lawyer, how people confront the questions of life helplessly, how they torment themselves for an explanation of one thing or another, and, in the end, resign themselves to the thought that we probably cannot arrive at a satisfactory answer. You yourself may well have had similar experiences. Therefore, if, as a seeker, one has had the inestimable good fortune to come upon this Message, then quite simply I consider it one's human duty to bring it to the attention of other seekers. For here, in penetratingly clear language, understandable to all, lies the help for our needs, the answer to our questions. I can assure you that whether you acquire this book, whether you read it or not, neither I nor anyone else has anything to gain. Nor—and today this must be emphatically stressed—will any sect seek to win you over. You alone are to draw benefit from this work. Only when you have recognized its value will people to whom the same has happened be prepared to help you deepen your insights insofar as you wish.

In any case, there is still something you would like to hear from me. The name of the author, which so far I have not mentioned. His name is Oskar Ernst Bernhardt, but he wrote this work under the name Abd-ru-shin. I have purposely not mentioned his name until now, for to be honest, of what use is this knowledge to you? When Jesus once walked the earth he had no other proof than His Word, than the Message that He brought.

He, the simple son of a carpenter from Nazareth, could not lay claim to any "prominence." Those who followed Him had to recognize Him by the importance of His teaching. Thus, the Author of this work also wrote:

"*Heed not the Bringer, but the Word!*"

If we consider it properly, ladies and gentlemen, this sentence contains a great deal. It brings something very different from the dim endeavors that nowadays are too often found under the pretext of "spiritual enlightenment." A true helper will never make his person the center of his teaching. I would like to say no more to you on this subject now. Otherwise I would rob you of an irretrievable experience of joy that awaits you with the serious study of this work.

With this study you set foot on the path to a conscious life. For as long as we are ignorant of our human spiritual nature, as long as we do not know our path and goal, then no matter how intellectually clever and learned we may be we are in truth blind and deaf. Unconscious of our own power and its interplay with the powers of this Creation, we move along apathetically, physically alive, but spiritually dead. Only with the recognition that we are interwoven in the working of Creation do we, and do things around us, visibly come to life, for the words of *The Grail Message* comes true:

"*You can immediately recognize that you really have the Word of Truth in my Message if you look around you wakefully, for your whole earth-life up till now, as well*

as the new experiencing of every moment,
both outwardly and inwardly, will become
completely clear to you as soon as you illumine
and regard it from my Message." . . . .

I hope I have succeeded in opening your eyes at least to a very small but extremely important section of the vitality of this Creation, and, at the same time, also to the vastness of our existence. Although we began with death we end with life, but with, I hope, a more conscious life. Thus I would like to take leave of you with that sentence with which the bringer of *The Grail Message* closed his foreword. It is the sentence that embraces our entire human task, reaching far beyond this earth-life, and which I would like to give you as my wish:

"*S**ee that you are truly alive in the wonderful Creation of your God!"* . . . .

If you have questions about the content of this lecture, please contact Reader Services at:

Grail Foundation Press
P. O. Box 45
Gambier, Ohio 43022
Telephone: 614.427-9410
Fax: 614.427-4954

Abd-ru-shin. 1990. *In the Light of Truth: The Grail Message.*
Stuttgart: Stiftung Gralsbotschaft

Heitler, Walter. 1963. *Man and Science.*
Oliver and Boyd.

Koestler, Arthur. *Der Mensch: Irrlaufer der Evolution.*
Bern/Munich: Scherz-Verlag

Moody, Raymond. 1988. *Life After Life.*
New York: Bantam Books, Inc.

*D**r. Richard Steinpach** was born in Vienna in 1917 where he was a lawyer for forty years. His professional life provided extensive opportunities to observe human nature, and to deal with many life-questions and problems. Between 1979 and 1991, he gave hundreds of lectures throughout Germany, Austria, and Switzerland. The powerful response of his audiences convinced him to publish his manuscripts in book form. In addition to* Why We Live After Death, *he also wrote several other books soon to be published by Grail Foundation Press, among them* How Can God Allow Such Things? *Dr. Steinpach died in 1992.*

In The Light Of Truth: The Grail Message
An Introduction

*I*N THE LIGHT OF TRUTH: THE GRAIL MESSAGE
is a classic work that offers clear and perceptive
answers to questions which challenge every human
being. Written between the years 1923-1938, it is
a collection of 168 lectures addressing all spheres of
life ranging from life after death to God and the Universe,
the Laws in Creation, free will, intuition and the intellect,
the ethereal world and the beyond, justice and love. It
answers eternal questions such as what does it mean to be
human, what is the purpose of life on earth, and what hap-
pens to "me" when I die. In the Light of Truth: The Grail
Message *explains the causes and significance of the unprece-*
dented crises facing humanity, and our responsibilities to the
future.

The author, Abd-ru-shin, was born in 1875 in Bischof-
swerda, Germany. His given name was Oskar Ernst Bern-
hardt. After being educated and trained in business, he
established himself in Dresden and became financially suc-
cessful. In the years that followed, he made many journeys
abroad, and wrote successful travel books, stories and plays.

After residing for some time in New York, Mr. Bernhardt
journeyed to England, and in 1913, moved to London.

There, the outbreak of World War I took him unawares, and in 1914 he was interned on the Isle of Man.

The seclusion of internment brought with it an inner deepening. He reflected continuously over questions connected with the meaning of life, birth and death, responsibility and free will, and with God and Creation. More and more the desire awakened within him to help humanity. He was released in the Spring of 1919 and returned to Germany.

In the 1920s, Abd-ru-shin gave public lectures. His explanation of the Knowledge of Creation resounded among his hearers. He began to write the first lectures for In the Light of Truth: The Grail Message *in 1923.*

In 1928, Abd-ru-shin settled in Austria on a mountain plateau called Vomperberg, where he continued writing The Grail Message. *The seizure of power in Austria by the Nazis in 1938 ended his work there. On March 12 of that year he was arrested, and his land and property were appropriated without compensation. In September, he was placed under house arrest, first in Schlauroth near Görlitz, and later in Kipsdorf in the Erzgebirge, where he was constantly under surveillance by the Gestapo. He was forbidden any further work for making* The Grail Message *known publicly.*

On December 6, 1941, Abd-ru-shin died from the effects of these measures.

In 1991, upon the fiftieth anniversary of his death, the Dresdner Nachrichten *newspaper published an article that included:*

*"*THE GRAIL MESSAGE, *which Oskar Ernst Bernhardt began to write in 1923 in Dresden, has now been translated*

into almost all the civilized languages of the western hemisphere, and is available ... around the globe. It was forbidden in the 'Third Reich,' but was also on the list of banned literature in East Germany. These periods of prohibition (in East Germany more than fifty years) markedly curtailed the possibility of disseminating The Grail Message *and making it known. One wonders why a non-political book like* The Grail Message *was still regarded by political systems as a 'source of danger.' The reason, perhaps, is that it sets up personal awareness of responsibility and individual freedom of choice against all conformity. Furthermore dogmatic limitations are alien to it, since it gives a comprehensive understanding, on the basis of the Laws of Creation, of the world and of life—beyond nationalities, races, and creeds."*

Concerning In the Light of Truth: The Grail Message, *Abd-ru-shin writes:*

> "I wish to fill the gaps which so far have remained unanswered in the souls of men as burning questions, and which never leave any serious thinker in peace."

Throughout The Grail Message *readers are urged to weigh questions and answers intuitively, to confront them within their own life experiences, and only to believe that which they can perceive inwardly. Only through this process can one reach true conviction in one's life.*

What follows is an abstract introducing some of the many principles contained in The Grail Message. *Full explanations are given within the work itself, and the brief discussion below can in no way substitute for the original.*

In the Light of Truth: The Grail Message *explains that human spirits emanated from the spiritual domain at the summit of Creation. God created the universe, and man is a part of that Creation. As such, God stands above Creation and man's place is within Creation. Creation has many different visible and invisible spheres of activity and substance. The meaning of human life on Earth and in the beyond is to develop spiritually so as to return to our primordial origin as fully conscious spirits.*

When a spirit comes to the material world for the first time in order to mature, it begins to make conscious choices for itself. Choices that do not swing with God's Laws burden the spirit with responsibility to redeem these choices either in the present lifetime, or in the spirit's subsequent reincarnations. Reincarnations provide spirits with direct opportunities to redeem the obligations they have created and to develop towards maturity.

God's Laws govern all of Creation, and, since human beings stand within Creation, these laws operate upon them whether or not they acknowledge this fact. Everything in Creation, without exception, is interconnected. Every circumstance in life is a result of the choices a spirit makes, and every circumstance is an opportunity to mature.

The Law of Motion: only with motion (vibrations) can there be life, and only with continual striving for ennoblement can there be ascent toward spiritual maturity. The higher one ascends, the faster and lighter are one's vibrations. The lower one descends, the slower and heavier are one's vibrations.

The Law of Gravity: everything that is noble, beautiful, pure or light produces an uplifting effect, while everything base, ignoble, or impure produces a sinking, dragging down effect. Therefore, after leaving this earth, every human being will enter that sphere that accords with its density. The Law of Gravity, combined with the Law of Attraction of Homogeneous Species, compels those of similar nature to be together.

The Law of Attraction of Homogeneous Species: like attracts like. Whatever emanates from a soul produces vibrations that take on forms corresponding exactly with their nature. Like forms attract each other, creating power centers that affect human beings according to their nature. When combined with the Law of Reciprocal Action, a single thought or action sent out returns strengthened by the Law of Attraction of Homogeneous Species.

The Law of Reciprocal Action: individuals reap what they sow; whatever emanates returns. Therefore, we are responsible for our every action and thought. If the action or thought is positive, then we ennoble Creation, and contribute to the advancement of the human race. If our actions or thoughts are negative, they bind us to whoever and whatever we harm, creating a karma that must be redeemed.

Individuals have free will. Each can decide whether or not to swing with the Laws in Creation, but the effects react upon them in either case. Human beings stand within Creation, and are responsible for their free choices. Man can only progress through an understanding of and adherence to these Laws.

Man's greatest error has been to place himself above God's Will. This arrogance has caused people to go forth blindly with destructive behavior, with thoughts and actions contrary to God's Will, thereby retarding their development toward spiritual maturity. The tool that human beings have most often misused is their intellect. They have overdeveloped the intellect at the cost of their intuition, their true spiritual connection. Indolence of spirit is a great weakness for many people, and the root cause of many of life's problems. This indolence has, over time, caused humans' spiritual abilities to become stunted through lack of use and has allowed the emergence of "intellectual mankind."

Within Creation, a multitude of helpers is available to us. Through the Laws of Creation, if an individual emanates pure thoughts and actions, they return strengthened and uplifted by similar thoughts and actions. We attract homogeneous species even more quickly and strongly from the unseen world. Everyone has guides, but most people have cut themselves off from these helps through the overdevelopment of their intellect and negligence of their intuition. Humans must learn to live harmoniously with each other and within Creation: this includes the world of nature.

Everything in Creation works in cycles (the Law of Motion). According to their nature, all cycles must end where they began. Human beings do not have unlimited opportunities for reincarnation in order to redeem karma and ascend spiritually. Only by swinging fully with God's Laws will we be able to continue our existence within Creation.

God's Justice, as seen in His constant, unvarying Laws, and His creation of humans in the first place, allowing us to live joyously in Creation and to ennoble that which is around us, gives evidence of His great Love.

In the Light of Truth: The Grail Message *is directed solely to the individual human being, irrespective of creed, nationality or race. It gives comprehensive explanations of the laws that govern the universe including the visible, material world and the various spheres through which the human spirit journeys on its return to its primordial origin. A work which will bring disquiet into many circles, its tone is uplifting, but severe. It requires that each individual is fully responsible for every action and thought produced, whether one accepts that responsibility or not.*

Other Titles from Grail Foundation Press

IN THE LIGHT OF TRUTH: THE GRAIL MESSAGE
•
THE TEN COMMANDMENTS OF GOD
THE LORD'S PRAYER
•
LAO-TSE

*available at your local bookstore
or directly through the publisher*

*Grail Foundation Press
P.O. Box 45
Gambier, OH 43022
1-800-427-9217*

Publisher's catalog available on request

IN THE LIGHT OF TRUTH: THE GRAIL MESSAGE
by Abd-ru-shin

In the Light of Truth: The Grail Message is a classic work that offers clear and perceptive answers to questions which challenge every human being. This collection of 168 essays addresses all spheres of life ranging from God and the Universe to the Laws in Creation, the meaning of life, responsibility, free will, intuition and the intellect, the ethereal world and the beyond, justice and love. *The Grail Message* will appeal to any human being who is seeking to understand life, his or her place in Creation, and the source of one's being.

Linen edition, three volumes combined
ISBN 1-57461-006-6
5.5" x 8.5"
1,062 pages
Paper edition, three-volume boxed set
ISBN 1-57461-003-1
6" x 9"
1,079 pages

Original edition: German
Translations available in:
Czech, Dutch, English, Estonian, French, Hungarian,
Italian, Portuguese, Rumanian, Russian,
Slovak, Spanish

THE TEN COMMANDMENTS OF GOD
THE LORD'S PRAYER
by Abd-ru-shin

Clearly explained in the full, life-embracing meaning, *The Ten Commandments of God and The Lord's Prayer* is a book for anyone striving to live with integrity. Readers who bring these Commandments to life within themselves will find they create a solid foundation for their daily lives and for their existence beyond physical death. Abd-ru-shin's insights regarding the Lord's Prayer help the reader understand this "key to the Kingdom of God" in its profound significance for mankind.

Linen edition
ISBN 1-57461-007-4
5" x 7.5"
72 pages
Paper edition
ISBN 1-57461-004-X
5" x 7.5"
72 pages

Original edition: German
Translations available in:
Czech, Dutch, English, French, Italian, Portuguese,
Russian, Slovak, Spanish

LAO-TSE
*The Life and Work
of the Forerunner in China*

Little is known about the life and work of this enlightened Chinese sage. In *Lao-Tse*, the personality of this leader and the events of his life are simply and clearly portrayed. The first in a series, this wonderful story was transcribed from the direct experience of living pictures taken from the Book of Life by one gifted to do so.

*Paper edition
ISBN 1-57461-008-2
6" x 9"
288 Pages*

*Original Edition: German
Translations available in:
Czech, English, French*